Journey One

A collection of images from Travel Photographer of the Year

Imagos – The Photographers' Press

Publisher / Editor / Author – Chris Coe
Editor / Author – Karen Coe
Designer Terry Steeley

First published by
Travel Photographer of the Year
PO Box 2716, Maidenhead, Berkshire, SL6 7ZN, UK

First edition published in 2005
ISBN 0-9549396-0-3 (paperback)
ISBN 0-9549396-1-1 (hardback)

Reproduced, printed and bound by Connekt Colour, Berkhamstead, HP4 1EH, UK
Designed by Iridius Design, Daventry, Northamptonshire, NN11 0SB, UK

Front cover photograph:
Salar de Uyuni, Bolivia © Ian Judd, Australia

Back cover photographs (clockwise from top left):
We are the world © Sam Lim Kien Hock, Malaysia
Blackpool, England © Chris Parker, UK
Monk with camera, Myanmar © Pete Adams, UK
Camel train in Sahara, Tunisia © Martin Brent, UK
Paradise Island, Malaysia © Pang Piow Kan, Malaysia

Frontispiece photograph:
Boy in trainers, Mali © Matjaz Krivic, Slovenia

Page 4 photograph:
Travelling with Joséphine, 6 months old – Zurich, Switzerland © Daniel Ross, Netherlands

The 'Journey' portfolios are a series of photographic adventures that will take you around the world through the eyes of many different photographers.

Journey One is the first in the series. It features the very best images from both the 2003 and 2004 Travel Photographer of the Year competitions; all the award-winning shots, plus some of the many others that merited publication. It's about the joy and excitement of travel and it's about life, culture, colour, people and this amazing planet. Whether you're a lover of travel or a lover of photography, the 'Journey' series will inspire you.

Travel photography encompasses many different subjects; people, landscapes, festivals, food, wildlife, places of interest, history, culture, tourism, leisure, adventure and more. Any aspect of life related to travel is a subject for travel photography. Capturing so many diverse elements requires great skill, and it's this creative talent and versatility that the Travel Photographer of the Year competition seeks to recognise and celebrate.

Choosing the images for Journey One was a difficult but inspiring task. The photographs on the following pages are just a small selection of the many that merited inclusion. We could literally have filled three books and it is heartbreaking to exclude so many good images, but every journey must start somewhere.

Travel is a passion for many of us. It gets into the blood. With every turn of the page, each 'Journey' portfolio will take you somewhere different; somewhere familiar or somewhere new. Each collection of beautiful and breathtaking images is the world viewed through someone else's eyes and, in a world where so much is brought to us in our homes, perhaps it will inspire you to travel and experience the sheer magic for yourself.

Everyone's a travel photographer. That's what we all do; we go to places and we take pictures. It's a way of capturing moments to share with other people who weren't there at the time.

There are so many fantastic places to go, people to meet and experiences to savour and, although the world seems to get smaller as travel becomes easier, there are still many locations that remain virtually unvisited and many that merit returning to.

Since the invention of photography over a century ago many travellers have recorded images of their journeys, the places they visited and cultures that they encountered. We take travel images for granted because they fill the printed page and the internet. Yet this accessibility has lead to a glut of images, perhaps even a lowering of standards of acceptable photography, and created a perception that anyone can take good travel photographs.

Of course there are many great travel images but there are many more poor ones, and too many where the photographer has taken the obvious shot, copied someone else's or simply just not been creative. After all, if we all take the same photographs then what's the point?

In 2003 a new annual international travel photography competition, Travel Photographer of the Year, was launched. The aim of the competition was to create a showcase for the very best in travel photography. It immediately fired the imagination of photographers around the world, attracting an entry of just under 10,000 images from photographers in 34 countries in its very first year. In 2004 the competition took another step forward with more entrants from more countries, but Travel Photographer of the Year is not just about numbers. The competition is structured to challenge photographers in every aspect of travel photography. It isn't easy to win and it's not designed to be.

The competition is open to anyone who takes photographs on their travels – to date the oldest entrant is 88 while the youngest is just six years old, and there are special awards for younger photographers. No distinction is made between amateur and professional photographers and neither should there be. Since when has someone's ability to earn a living from taking photographs made them a better photographer than a good amateur enthusiast? Poor photography is no more the domain of the beginner than real creative talent is the domain of the pro.

Neither is the competition just about the winners, as this book clearly shows. Most of these images were taken by entrants who didn't win but it would be hard to argue that they are any less memorable than the winning ones.

Travel Photographer of the Year is run by photographers for photographers. Over the years we hope to challenge and encourage photographers to be more creative, and we hope to nurture new talent and raise the awareness of travel photography in its own right through the competition, this book, subsequent 'Journey' portfolios and our exhibitions. In return our entrants can put something back into the communities that they photograph by supporting our chosen tourism-related charities each year.

The work of over 160 photographers fills the following pages and all the images were entered into the competition in 2003 or 2004. They were taken by photographers from around the world, amateur and professional, young and old. We would like to thank these photographers, and all the other competition entrants, who have made this book possible.

If you have a camera, or can borrow one, then we hope that their wonderful images will inspire you to start or to improve your photography, so that in years to come you can share your images with the world. It doesn't matter whether your travels are short or long, take a journey...

TRAVEL PHOTOGRAPHER
OF THE YEAR 2004

This title is usually awarded to the photographer who submits the best two portfolios in different categories. However the standard of the winning photographer Pang Piow Kan's work in 2004 was so consistently high that images from three of his portfolios have been included in this book.

Sponsors of this prize:

Star Alliance   Calumet Photographic   Adobe

Bajau tribes children, transporting themselves around their water village, Umadal Island, Sipadan Marine Park, Sabah, Malaysia. Pang Piow Kan, Malaysia

Mabul Island, Sabah, Malaysia. Pang Piow Kan, Malaysia

Arriving at the Sipadan Marine Park, Sabah, Malaysia. Pang Piow Kan, Malaysia

TRAVEL PHOTOGRAPHER OF THE YEAR 2004

Pang Piow Kan Malaysia
Winner

Amateur photographer Pang Piow Kan became interested in photography in 1983, when he began photographing his young children. Stung by criticism of his images from his friends, he became determined to prove them wrong and worked to improve his skills.

He slowly grew to appreciate the art of photography and discovered a not inconsiderable talent. Pang Piow Kan is retired, and his photography is a hobby which brings him great joy and which has also secured him international success in photographic competitions.

He occasionally gives photographic lessons and lectures to local and overseas photographic societies, sharing his experience and his love of travel and photography.

"Travelling is enriching for me as not only do I get to learn and photograph other cultures, I have made many friends overseas. Be it seminars, or photo excursions, it is a privilege to share it with my students and see them create their own style."

Balinese releasing flowers into the lake for morning prayers, Pedugul Lake, Bali, Indonesia. Pang Piow Kan, Malaysia

Balinese family carrying their offerings to the temple for prayers, Bali, Indonesia. Pang Piow Kan, Malaysia

Black-naped Oriole feeding its young, Penang, Malaysia Pang Piow Kan, Malaysia

A Stork-Billed Kingfisher catching fish for its young, Oil Palm Estate, Penang Malaysia. Pang Piow Kan, Malaysia

YOUNG TRAVEL PHOTOGRAPHER OF THE YEAR 2004

My World, My View: Anna Scott's remarkable images were taken during a three-month long holiday through Indonesia to Western Australia. Not only do they demonstrate a great talent for capturing the moment, but in several of the images there is an intimacy which an adult would find hard, if not impossible, to capture. This portfolio is a personal view extremely well interpreted.

Sponsors of this prize:

Light & Land   Hewlett Packard   Adobe

A 'clown' or marshal attempts to retrieve a horse that has thrown its rider, Halls Creek Rodeo, Kimberley, Western Australia. Anna Scott, UK

Sea water thrown onto the sand will evaporate in the sun leaving salt crystals for collection, western Bali. Anna Scott, UK

YOUNG TRAVEL PHOTOGRAPHER
OF THE YEAR 2004

Anna Scott UK
Winner

Although Anna has lived with photography all her life (her father is a professional photographer) she is a relative newcomer to getting behind the camera herself. In fact it was only when her grandparents bought her a Canon A70 as a present to take away on a three month trip through Indonesia and the Kimberley region of Western Australia that she started taking photography seriously. However, showing the typical determination with which she approaches all challenges, she threw herself into learning how to use the camera and before long was addicted.

All four pictures in her portfolio were taken on this trip, between April and July 2003, when she was aged 12. Her natural curiosity, eye for an image and sensitivity with people made up for her lack of technical knowledge during this period, enabling her to produce a number of striking images that many longer standing photographers would be proud of.

As well as photography Anna also loves writing and travelling. She hopes to combine all three one day to earn a living.

Members of a family gather to meet visitors in the centre of a traditional village in central Flores, Indonesia. Anna Scott, UK

PEOPLES AND CULTURES PORTFOLIO 2004

More than simply portraits, Peoples and Cultures was designed to show humanity and the cultures that make us who we are. In his winning portfolio, Remi Benali's images intimately touch the culture. They were taken in and around the ancient library of the desert in Chinguetti, Mauritania, and sensitively convey the influence that their surroundings exert on the people he has photographed.

Sponsors of this prize:
Guerba   Fujifilm   Adobe

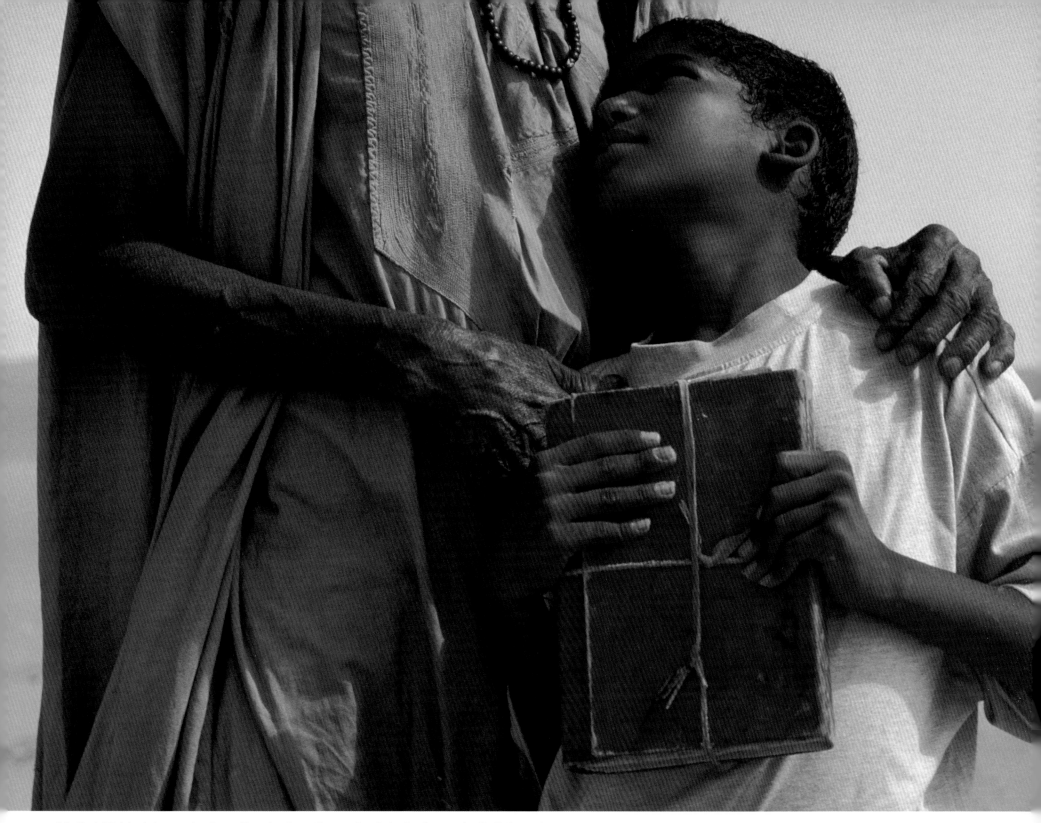

Abdarahim Ould Beja hands down an antique Koran to his grandson Hassan. The manuscript collections have been passed on like this for centuries. Remi Benali, France

PEOPLES AND CULTURES

Remi Benali France
Winner

After receiving a diploma in economics and a law degree, French photographer Remi Benali started his career in 1990. He worked with the photo agency Gamma for twelve years, including three years as a foreign press correspondent in the United States. He is currently independent.

His journeys have led him to over 60 countries – from the Russian North Pole to the Sahara Desert, from the remote jungles of Sumatra to the Indian rituals in the Andes mountains. His personal work celebrates the living remnants of a vanishing past, with a focus on rituals and traditions, tribal cultures and UNESCO World Heritage sites in peril.

An award-winning photographer (including the Pictures of the Year Competition in 1997 and an Award of Excellence 2003 by Communication Arts), Remi Benali's work has appeared in numerous international publications such as Time, Life, Newsweek, the Sunday Times, Paris-Match, Stern, Geo (German, Spanish and Korean editions), El Pais, El Mundo, La Repubblica Delle Donne, Specchio, Le Figaro magazine and National Geographic Adventure.

Ahmed Ould Wenane, one of the curators of the centuries-old libraries in Chinguetti, Mauritania. Remi Benali, France

Mint Homode, curator of the Ouadane library. Remi Benali, France

One of the ancient manuscripts of the libraries of the desert in Chinguetti, Mauritania. Remi Benali, France

High on the Tibetan plateau, a prayer wheel spins in the hands of a believer. Litang, Sichuan Province, China. Will Salter, Australia

Another day comes to a close at the Jinsuo Dao market, Yunnan Province, China. Will Salter, Australia

PEOPLES AND CULTURES

Will Salter Australia
Runner Up

There's a fascinating mix of photographic skills displayed in Will's images combined with a keen eye for a strong composition. His images observe an intriguing but fading culture without intruding on it.

A traditional Naxi woman at Tiger Leaping Gorge, Yunnan, China. Will Salter, Australia

The dramatic and rapid modernisation of China encroaches on the traditions of old. Kunming, Yunnan Province. Will Salter, Australia

投资、创业、生活
心动不如行动

A fisherman approaches the village of Kolenze on the Niger River, Mali. Remi Benali, France

PEOPLES AND CULTURES

Remi Benali France
Highly Commended

Remi uses bold composition and a sense of scale and proportion to great effect in these photographs. There is something both dramatic and engaging about this style that draws you into his images.

Great Mosque of Djenné, Mali, the largest clay monument in the world, listed on the UNESCO World Heritage List. Remi Benali, France

In this village in Kerala, India all the houses had family pictures displayed in the front (open) room. Marco Pozzi, UK

Yoga teacher in yoga school at Rishikesh, India. Marco Pozzi, UK

PEOPLES AND CULTURES

Marco Pozzi UK
Commended

There's a strong technical quality to Marco's work which compliments his ability
to engage with his subjects. The eye contact gives his portraits a deeply personal
edge yet there is something unusually stoic about them.

ESSENCE OF TRAVEL PORTFOLIO 2004

Travel has many flavours and colours. The Essence of Travel is about capturing those elements that encapsulate a travel experience. Chris Parker chose the English seaside resort of Blackpool as his travel experience and has captured it brilliantly with bold composition and vibrant colour.

Sponsors of this prize:
Discover The World   Hasselblad   Adobe

Blackpool, Lancashire, England. Chris Parker, UK

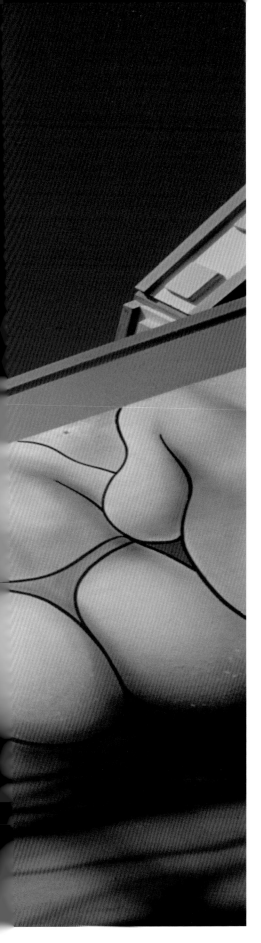

Blackpool, Lancashire, England. Chris Parker, UK

ESSENCE OF TRAVEL

Chris Parker UK
Winner

Chris Parker is based in the historic Cinque Port of Hastings on the East Sussex coast of England and has been a freelance photographer for twenty years. A regular travel writer and photographer for Woman's Weekly magazine, Chris has won a host of national and international awards for his work. He travels the world on behalf of commercial clients, while in the UK he is often commissioned by local government clients and regional tourist boards. He has also been an accredited Royal Press Photographer on two overseas tours.

His career as a photographer began when he was working as a cartoonist for a postcard company. They needed to update their range of London and South East England photographs, so he borrowed a camera and spent the next few years learning the ropes.

He claims to have a love/hate relationship with photography – "Sometimes everything goes wrong – the weather's awful, lorries park right in front of you, a group of comedians stand in front of your camera and crack the old, old jokes about David Bailey. Yet every now and then I still get immense satisfaction when everything falls into place and a shoot goes way beyond expectations."

Chris's love of travel has clearly been inherited by his young daughter – aged just 11, she is soon to have her first travel feature published.

Blackpool, Lancashire, England. Chris Parker, UK

Tourists on horseback leaving Mount Bromo, East Java, Indonesia. Arthur Teng, Malaysia

Early morning scene of active Mount Bromo, East Java, Indonesia. Arthur Teng, Malaysia

Horsemen waiting for tourists at the foot of Mount Bromo, East Java, Indonesia. Arthur Teng, Malaysia

ESSENCE OF TRAVEL

Arthur Teng Malaysia
Runner Up

You get a real feel for the journey in Arthur's beautifully shot portfolio of the Indonesian island of Java. The early morning light is majestic and his images tell the story of a special place.

A horse near a Hindu temple at Candi Gedung Songo in Central Java, Indonesia. Arthur Teng, Malaysia

Jetty at Kandholhudoo, Spa Resort Island, South Ari Atoll, Maldives. Felix Hug, Australia

Preparing the flowers to decorate the spa, Kuramathi Island, South Ari Atoll, Maldives. Felix Hug, Australia

ESSENCE OF TRAVEL

Felix Hug Australia
Highly Commended

There's a serenity in Felix's images which belies the subtle composition and clever use of low light in this portfolio. Fantastic photography and a dream destination. Don't you just wish you were there?

ESSENCE OF TRAVEL

Felix Hug Australia
Commended

A complete contrast in styles in Felix's second portfolio shows a keen eye for an interesting and unusual image. The trackside market may look like a tumbled down accident but produce is precisely placed by the stall owners. This is a good photographic study of human adaptability in less than favourable conditions.

Street scene in Vientiane, Laos. Felix Hug, Australia

City market in Samut Songkram, North of Bangkok Thailand. The train runs through the stalls several times a day. Felix Hug, Australia

Mud volcano, Columbia. Glen Howey, New Zealand. This image is part of Glen's Highly Commended portfolio.

SPIRIT OF ADVENTURE PORTFOLIO 2004

Adventure can be extreme but however large or small a particular challenge, the spirit must shine through. Alexander Nesbitt's images of a caravan across the Egyptian desert manage to capture his adventure in a portfolio of beautiful photographs which at the same time successfully portrays the harshness of the desert environment.

Sponsors of this prize:

Land Rover Resolutions Adobe

Dharb el Dakhla, the desert track to Dakhla oasis, Egyptian western desert. Alexander Nesbitt, USA

SPIRIT OF ADVENTURE

Alexander Nesbitt USA
Winner

Alexander 'Sandy' Nesbitt's interest in photography was sparked when he took a photo 101 class during his second year in art school. Taking night shots near his (then) home on the lower east side of Manhattan caused that spark to become a flame and he discovered a love of depicting the real world through his camera, rather than through painting or sculpture. He made the decision to turn professional in 1997 after returning from a volunteer season on a dig in Egypt, and three years later photography had become his full-time career.

Now residing both in New York and Newport, Rhode Island – where he operates his storefront studio/gallery under the name Blink Gallery – he works in documentary, adventure travel, commercial and fashion photography.

His work has taken him across the world. It allows him to communicate his passion for life and for adventure, and he relishes the challenge of creating an image that conveys a particular theme or message. A keen interest in the truth

of situations and simple, communicative images that reveal them is the source of inspiration for his photo-journalistic work as well as his travel work. His photographic 'heroes' include Nachtway, Salgado, Raghbir Singh, Mary Ellen Mark, Mike Yamashita, Eugene Richards, and Steve McCurry

Whilst his native America gives wonderful opportunities for photography, he finds that the outsider's perspective he has when working outside the US keeps him observant, giving

his work an extra edge. Although he comes from a family of great travellers, he prefers to work alone. While lonely and at times difficult, it allows him to follow his hunches and instincts without distraction and to be more accessible to the people he photographs.

Checking route and position. Dharb el Dakhla, the desert track to Dakhla oasis, Egyptian western desert. Alexander Nesbitt, USA

On foot for four days, with six still to go. Dharb el Dakhla, the desert track to Dakhla oasis, Egyptian western desert. Alexander Nesbitt, USA

Day break brings the ritual of tea boiled on a tiny fire. Dharb el Dakhla, the desert track to Dakhla oasis, Egyptian western desert. Alexander Nesbitt, USA

SPIRIT OF ADVENTURE

Martin Hartley UK
Runner Up

What do you do with all that ice and snow? It can't be easy to find interesting and varied images while taking photographs in such extreme and featureless conditions yet Martin has found four strikingly different ways to portray the epic struggle of a polar explorer. His images convey the enormity of the challenge.

Far right: Cornwallis Island, Canadian High Arctic: Pen Hadow, the first person in history to walk to the North Pole from North America completely unsupported. Martin Hartley, UK

Polar explorers swim in one-piece waterproof suits to reach the North Pole, Cornwallis Island, Canadian High Arctic. Martin Hartley, UK

Resolute Bay, High Arctic: Polar adventurers wear skis to dissipate their weight. Sometimes the ice they tread upon is only a few centimetres thick. Martin Hartley, UK

Wetboy, Burning Man, Nevada, USA. Anthony Pletts, UK

Dustbird, Burning Man, Nevada, USA. Anthony Pletts, UK

SPIRIT OF ADVENTURE

Anthony Pletts UK
Joint Highly Commended

Good photographers think creatively and Anthony's interpretation of the spirit of adventure admirably demonstrates the lateral thinking that this category deserves. We don't all trek across the desert or undertake polar expeditions but we all have adventures. These images show a very human adventure with humour and spirit.

Petra, Jordan. Glen Howey, New Zealand

Toule Sap, Cambodia. Glen Howey, New Zealand

SPIRIT OF ADVENTURE

Glen Howey New Zealand
Joint Highly Commended

Would you like to travel with Glen? Caked in mud and shot at, it's not everyone's idea of fun, but these very different adventures are well photographed, combining a sense of danger with humour, good observation and an ability to capture the moment.

LIVING PLANET
PORTFOLIO 2004

This is a planet of seemingly boundless beauty and diversity.
In her Living Planet portfolio, Daisy Gilardini has managed
to convey power, movement, humour and extremes of
temperature through stunning wildlife and landscape images.
The image of the volcano erupting plays tricks on the eyes and
has a strangely hypnotic quality, capturing the very essence
of the living planet.

Sponsors of this prize:

G.A.P Adventures   Wacom   Adobe

A group of Spotted Petrels, Antarctic Peninsula. Daisy Gilardini, Switzerland

Details of a very old iceberg, Antarctica. Daisy Gilardini, Switzerland

LIVING PLANET

Daisy Gilardini Switzerland
Winner

Daisy Gilardini is based in Lugano – Ticino, the sunshine state of Switzerland. She started taking photography seriously during her first trip to India in 1989 and since then has visited more than 30 countries with camera in hand.

By 1999 she was selling her photography. Her work has been published in some of the best travel magazines in Europe such as Animan, Newland and Airone, and her images are regularly used for calendars, postcards and puzzles. Two of her images were highly honoured in the American 'Nature's Best' photo contest in 2003.

For Daisy, photography means extreme adventure, "Being a nature and animal lover, I always choose remote destinations.

The mystery of these wild places, the force of nature and isolation from civilization combined with extreme adventure, are simply irresistible for me. As a woman I've never been fussy and I have the ability to adapt to any surroundings. I can also sleep anywhere. In my mind, logistical or physical difficulties pale in comparison to the beauty of the places I visit.

"Travel for me is synonymous with adventure and it serves my desire to break the monotony of daily routine. I don't take pictures in order to have the best photo to sell; my photographs come from the heart. I take photographs to stay connected with nature and animals, and to share exceptional moments with special people – these are the things I love most in my life."

A laughing Weddell Seal, Antarctica. Daisy Gilardini, Switzerland

Leaves of the flax plant, Stewart Island, New Zealand. David Hill, UK

LIVING PLANET

David Hill UK
Runner Up

Capturing detail in effective compositions is a skill which eludes many photographers but Dave has mastered it with a wonderfully subtle and understated study of the natural world.

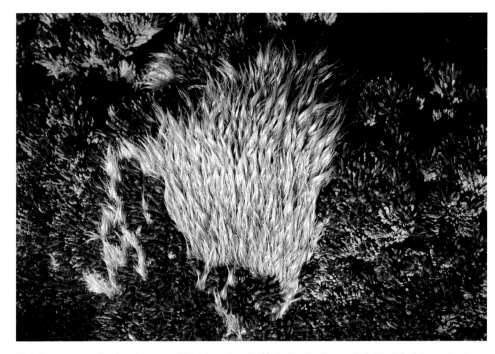

A tuft of grass seems to flare from the embers of the rock-hugging plant life. Rocky Point, Stewart Island, New Zealand. David Hill, UK

Bleached wood of stunted Manukau trees, Stewart Island, New Zealand. David Hill, UK

These surreal 'trees' are caused by runnels of water eroding the sand on a beach to expose a darker layer beneath. Stewart Island, New Zealand. David Hill, UK

LIVING PLANET

Julie Rémy Canada
Highly Commended

Julie's cleverly constructed portfolio is themed using different natural shapes and colours to link details, larger landscapes and wildlife images. This approach allowed her to play with lines and textures while mixing close up and distant images.

Riverflow colours, Kennedy River, British Columbia, Canada. Julie Rémy, Canada

Early morning jogging at Zabriskie Point, Death Valley National Park, California, USA. Julie Rémy, Canada

Furious wave, San Francisco Bay, California, USA. Qui Tan Le, USA

Moving rocks, Racetrack Playa, Death Valley National Park, California, USA. Qui Tan Le, USA

LIVING PLANET

Qui Tan Le USA
Commended

The forces of nature are predominant in Qui Tan Le's images. You can not begin to imagine the natural forces that have moved the two rocks across the parched ground to meet and yet this landscape looks so tranquil.

CELEBRATION
SINGLE IMAGE 2004

With a brief to capture an uplifting moment, the Celebration theme is a photographer's dream. It's all about one defining moment and that is exactly what Mark Edward Harris has captured in his winning shot of children somersaulting off a sea wall in the Marshall Islands. Everything is there – exuberance in perfect symmetry.

Sponsors of this prize:
Islands of the Bahamas   Adobe

CELEBRATION

Mark Edward Harris USA
Winner

Los Angeles-based Mark Edward Harris' first published photograph was in Peterson's Photographic – he received $25 for a shot of St. Basil's Cathedral in Moscow when he was nineteen. He started his 'real' professional photography career doing the stills for the Merv Griffin Show and various television and movie companies.

In 1986 he set off on a four-month trek across the Pacific and throughout South East Asia, China and Japan. The images created on that trip brought attention to his travel/documentary photography. He has since visited and photographed seventy countries.

His editorial work has appeared in publications including Life, Stern, American Photo, Black & White, Outdoor Photographer, Islands, The New York Times, The London Times, Playboy, Vogue, Elle, People, and The Los Angeles Times Sunday Magazine as well as many in-flight magazines.

Mark's commercial clients range from The Gap to cruise lines and airlines. He is the recipient of numerous awards including a CLIO Award and an Aurora Gold Award for his photographic work and an Ace Award for directing and producing a video for television.

His first solo exhibition was held at the Nikon Salon in Japan in 1992. Mark's book 'Faces of the Twentieth Century: Master Photographers and Their Work' – recording in words and pictures many of the great names in photography – won the prestigious New York Book Show 'Photography Book of the Year' and 'Best of Show' awards. His second book, 'The Way of the Japanese Bath,' a documentary/fine art look at Japanese hot springs, has been featured in magazines worldwide. Mark's latest book Wanderlust was released in November 2004.

Children performing aerobatics off a sea wall on the tiny atoll of Majuro in the Marshall Islands. Mark Edward Harris, USA

A young boy celebrates the arrival of a cool breeze during the hot season in Kolenze, Mali. Remi Benali, France

CELEBRATION

Remi Benali France
Runner Up

It's so hot. Feel that breeze! Remi's image needs no words – it is simply stunning.

CELEBRATION

Philip Lee Harvey UK
Highly Commended

Lost in the moment, Philip has captured the pure joy that
binds so many people to their religion in a world where it can
be the cause of, or excuse for, so much suffering.

CELEBRATION

Andrew Parkinson UK
Commended

Celebration takes many forms and is best when shared.
Andrew's image (on page 48) is wonderfully simple. You can
feel the cool water and sense the humour in the interaction
between man and animal.

Women celebrate a rite of fertility by turning 104 times around a sacred banyan tree in front of the Matangeshwara temple, Kajuraho, India. Remi Benali, France

21st Century Monk, Western Gate, Amarbayasgalant Monastery, Mongolia. Sebastian Pearson, UK

2004 STUDENT AWARDS

Three photographers with very different styles were judged the best student entries. Amanda Thomson's image of a baseball match shows an interesting documentary approach while Julie Rémy's tight composition was part of her highly commended Living Planet portfolio. The third award goes to Sam Scott for his vibrant use of movement and keen eye. Sam, aged 12, is also the youngest student to win this award.

Sponsors of this prize:
Plastic Sandwich

Wrigley Field, Chicago, USA. Amanda Thomson, UK

Bighorn sheep, Medicine Lake, Alberta, Canada. Julie Rémy, Canada

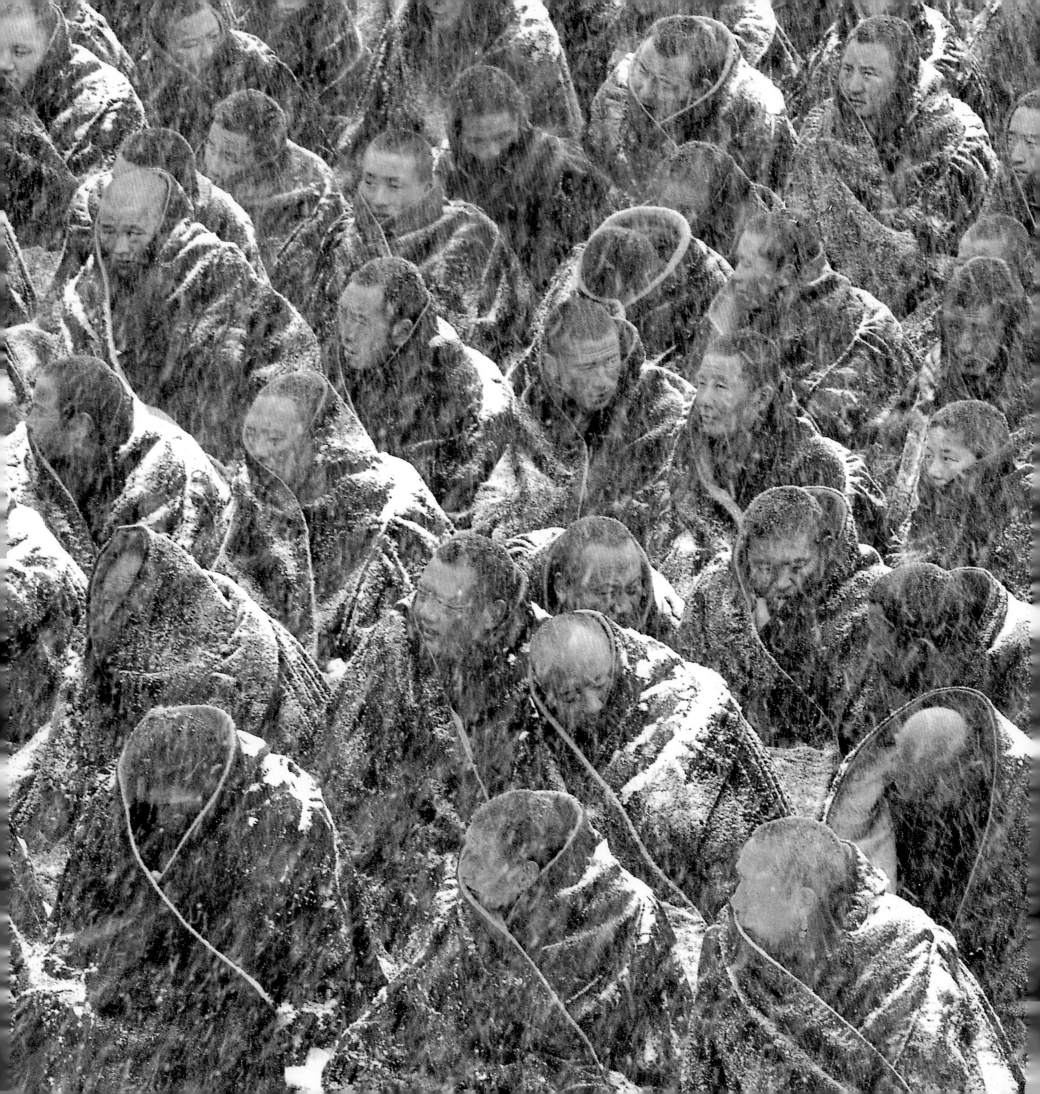

Travelling On...

Five days later and we're inching up the road from Pai to the 2175m hilltop of Doi Chiang Dao at 5am. Another unique attraction of our trusty Jeep is the erratic nature of the headlights, which is great fun as we navigate the switchback curves in the darkness. This is the second time we've done this, yesterday we made the four-hour round journey just to peer into the swirling cloud. This morning we're in cloud again as we climb, but looking straight up I can see the occasional star; we may be able to get above this mist.

Finally, up at the top the first mauves of twilight are colouring the sky to the east over a sea of mist. Isolated hills and trees stand clear.

It is indescribably beautiful.

Once again, I'm rushing to get set up in the half-light of dawn. Here we go again. Pause. Look out over the endless banks of cloud stretching across north-eastern Thailand to the Lao border. Reflect.

20 years ago this month I went freelance. Maybe I should have got a proper job, but for now, this will do.

David Noton, a passionate traveller and one of Britain's finest contemporary travel and stock photographers.

Polar bear, Churchill, Canada. Louise Drew, UK

Polar bear on ice, Spitzbergen, Norway. Staffan Widstrand, Sweden

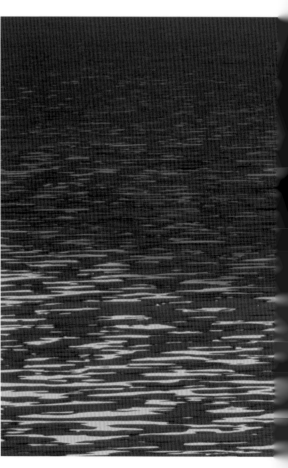

Midnight sun, Baffin Island, Canada. Staffan Widstrand, Sweden

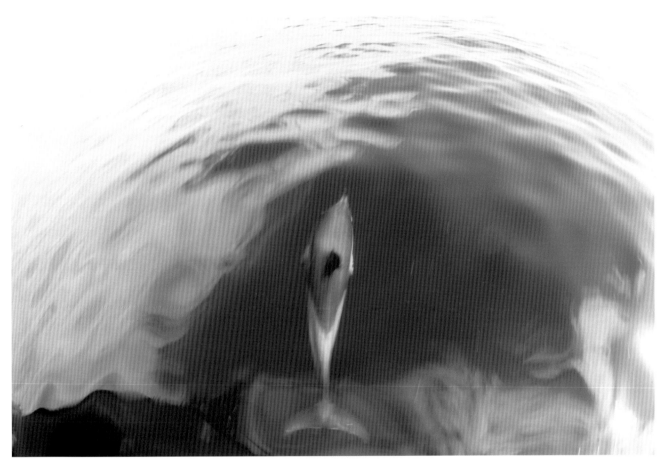

Common dolphin bow riding, The Azores. Gavin Parsons, UK

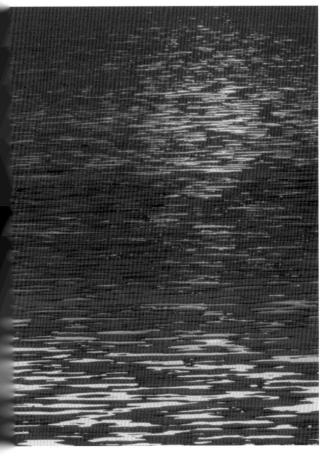

Dead Sea, Jordan. Conor Caffrey, Ireland

Hoi An Nets, Vietnam. Antonia Deutsch, UK.

Los Dios de los Muertos, Todos Santos, Guatemala. Lisa Wiltse, Australia

Tea time, Yukuin, Japan. Mark Edward Harris, USA

Weapons or toys, Sapa, Vietnam. Chris Kewish, UK

Kayaking in Bahia Los Angeles, USA. Guy Moberly, Spain

Old man playing, China. Richard Dutkowski, UK

Young man, Altiplano, Bolivia. Rory Carnegie, UK

Cape Verde, Newfoundland, Canada. Craig Easton, UK

A classic view reminiscent of a mediaeval oil painting, Grand Canal, Venice, Italy. Neil Warner, Ireland

A new day dawns in old Stone Town, Zanzibar, Tanzania. Stephen Garrett, Australia

Dusk in Djemma el Fna, Marrakech, Morocco. Domen Grögl, Slovenia

Hassan II Mosque, Casablanca, Morocco. Daniel Clements, UK

Onlookers watch ash jetting out of Etna's upper flanks, Sicily, Italy. Jeremy Bishop, UK

White water rafting on the Zambezi, Zambia. Paul Goldstein, UK

Suspension bridge in Hunza Valley, Pakistan. Alessandra Meniconzi, Switzerland

Mosque Agadez, Niger. Peter Dixon, UK

Tuk tuk ride, Chiang Mai, Thailand. Krystyn den Hertog, Ireland

'Evolution', Angel underground station, London, England. Geoff Crawford, UK

Trevose Head, Cornwall, England. Craig Easton, UK

Selim River, Kedah, Malaysia. Pang Piow Kan, Malaysia

Hang glider, Verbier, Switzerland. Martin Brent, UK

Campervan, The Marina, West Kirby, England. Craig Easton, UK

Sailingboat on Loch Dunvegan, Isle of Skye, Scotland. Arthur Sevestre, Netherlands

Early morning, Qinghai, Western China. Jeremy Browne, UK

4am on an April morning, tide rushing in, Norfolk, England. Ian Aitken, UK

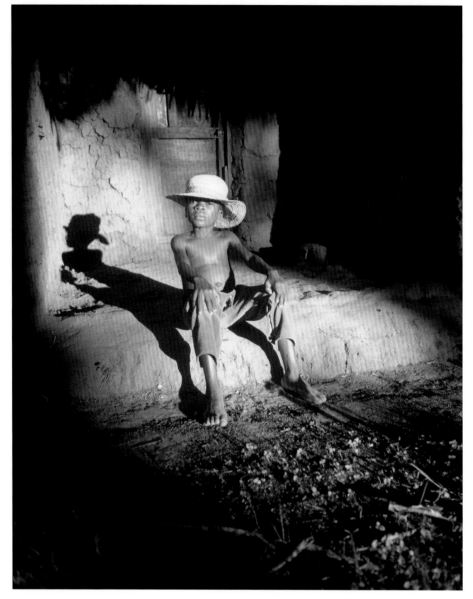

Komba, Tanzania. Derek Charlwood, UK

Take off from Reagan National Airport, Washington DC, USA. Chris Usher, USA

The eldest daughter of a coffee picking family, Ahuachapan, El Salvador. Benjamin Rusnak, USA

Indian bus stop. Kurt Tong, UK

Back alley foodstall, Tokyo, Japan. James Reeve, UK

Taking a break, Chengdhu, Sichuan Province, China. Mike Stone, Australia

Children playing hopping game, Monjo School, Sagarmartha National Park, Nepal. Tiffany Peen, UK

Beach bum, Costa de La Luz, Spain. Michelle Chaplow, Spain

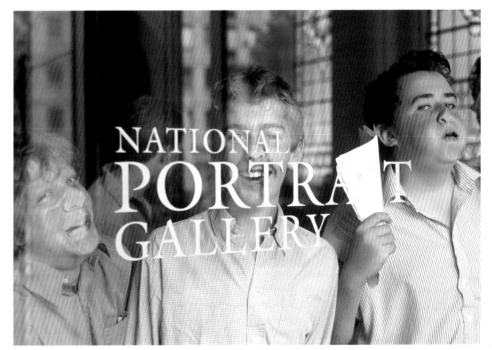

National Portrait Gallery, London, England. Ian Moore, UK

Wild horses in a blizzard, Wales. Martin Phillips, UK

Lady in green, India. Marco Pozzi, UK

Blue seascape between storms, Isle of Skye, Scotland. Steve Wright, UK

A dragonfly on a blade of grass, Bali, Indonesia. LaRose Benedict, USA

European tree frog, La Brenne, France. Jeroen Mentens, Belgium

Royal National Park, New South Wales, Australia. Marc Anderson, Spain

Zebra at dawn, Namibia. Teresa Schiappa, Portugal

Schooling Barracuda, Sipadan. Shaun Tierney, UK

Pontoon bridges over the River Ganges at dawn, Allahabad, India. Armar Grover, UK

Mushroom coral, Great Barrier Reef, Australia. Merridy Cairn-Duff, Australia

Opera House, Sydney, Australia. Martin Brent, UK

The Infinity Pool at Soneva Gili Resort, Maldive Islands. Frances Howorth, UK

Motorbikes in Saigon, Vietnam. Tim Hall, UK

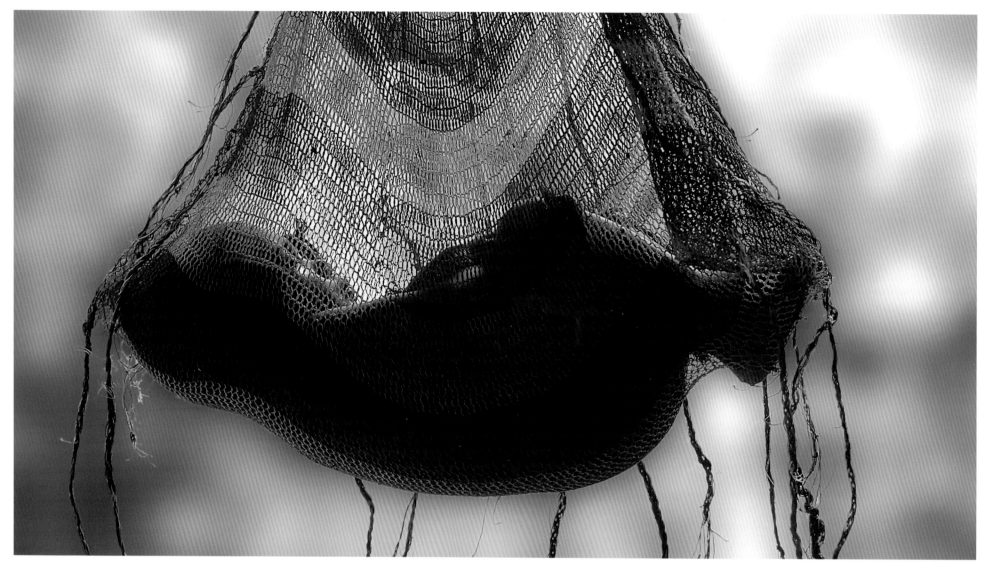

Baby in a Billium bag, New Guinea. Kieron Nelson, Canada

Romeria del Rocio pilgrimage, Andalucia, Spain. Ian Aitken, UK

Stag silhouette, UK. Andrew Parkinson, UK

Lioness, Tanzania. Philip Lee Harvey, UK

Palm tree in stormy weather, California, USA. Ellen Clark, USA

Tourist camel ride in Erg Chebbi, Sahara Desert, Morocco. Gary Cook, UK

Checkers, Makadui Trading Post near Mbale, Uganda. Richard Sobol, USA

Chefchaoeun, Morocco. Kim Taylor, UK

Northern Lights, Denali National Park, Alaska. Kennan Ward, USA

Risso's Dolphin, Monterey Bay, California, USA. Matthew Watkinson, UK

Double crested cormorant, Florida Everglades National Park, USA. Ben Murphy, USA

Maasai warrior hunting party, Masai Mara, Kenya. Matjaz Krivic, Slovenia

Kasbah, Sanaa, Yemen. William Bloomhuff, USA

Camel or bike, edge of the Sahara. Celia Mannings, UK

Women harvesting salt in Nha Trang, Vietnam. Jennifer Dunlop, UK

Storm, Mongolia. Clint Lucas, Dubai

Wild baby Macaque monkey, Sepilok, Borneo. Celia Mannings, UK

A young Sadhu and meditating guru, Maha Kumbh Mela, Allahabad, India. Karoki Lewis, UK

Shopping, Bogota, Columbia. Glen Howey, New Zealand

Tuareg tribesman, Algeria. Keith Kimber, UK

The esteemed old doctor of Quan Lan Island, Vietnam. Will Salter, Australia

Uluru Red Center, Australia. Martin Brent, UK

Himba boy with cup, Kaokoland, Namibia. Alexander Nesbitt, USA

After the rains in Hiddenvlei, Namibia. Janet Edwards, UK

Apricots laid out to dry, Karimabad, Hunza Valley, Pakistan. Jamie Marshall, UK

Corcovado, Rio de Janeiro, Brazil. John Pennock, UK

Mother and child, Chichicastenango, Guatemala. Peter Netley, UK

The giant Brihat Samrat Yantra sundial of the 18th century Jantar Mantar observatory, Jaipur, India. Ben Murphy, USA

Desert dawn, Namib Desert, Namibia. Nicola Jennet, UK

Surma tribesman, Mursi Hana, Omo Valley, Ethiopia. Guy Marks, UK

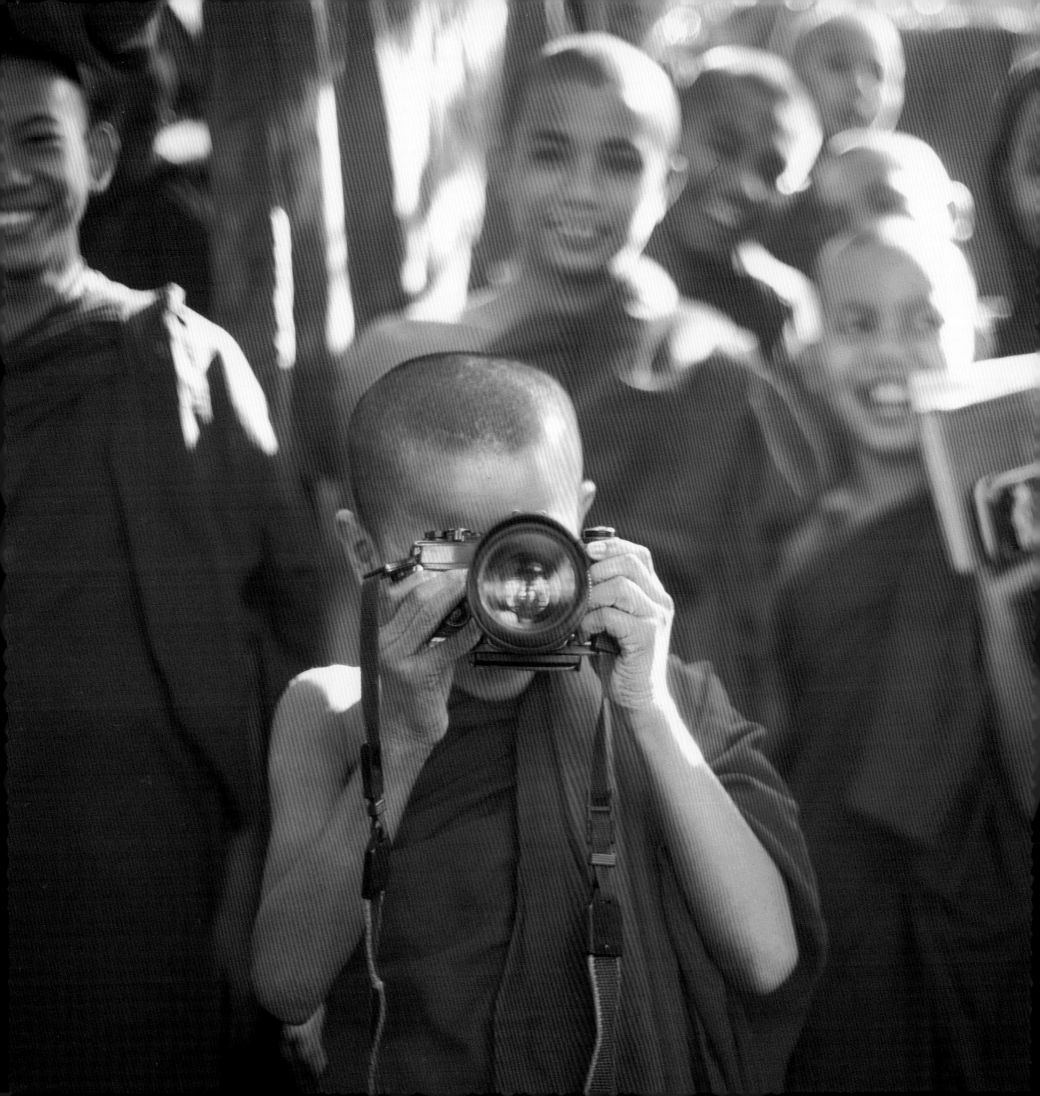

TRAVEL PHOTOGRAPHER OF THE YEAR 2003

Peter Adams' images from his People and Places and Colour and Passion portfolios made him a worthy winner of the first Travel Photographer of the Year award and set the benchmark for future years. They demonstrate the range of ability and the consistently high standard that the award was designed to recognise, combined with original ideas and a creativity that makes his work distinctive.

Sponsors of this prize:

Islands of the Bahamas   Calumet Photographic   Adobe   Lowepro

Lifeguard hut, Miami Beach, USA. Peter Adams, UK

TRAVEL PHOTOGRAPHER OF THE YEAR 2003

Peter Adams UK
Winner

Travel Photographer of the Year 2003, Peter Adams, originally studied Land Management at Southampton. He tried working as an estate agent but did not fit the groove! An independent spirit and a good photographic eye prompted him to start his own photographic business in 1986 with the help of a £40 per week government Enterprise Allowance grant. Initially he worked for design studios, advertising agencies and corporate clients.

A great love of the countryside and of travel inspired a move into travel photography. Despite having no formal training, Peter gradually built up an income and is now in the enviable position of being able to dedicate himself to full-time travel photography.

Specialising in stock photography, Peter now has an extensive photo library and has travelled to over 40 countries. His shots are regularly seen as poster prints, cards, CD covers and in books, magazines and calendars. He has produced calendars for such companies as Canon and SmithKline Beecham.

Peter was born in London and when in England he is now based on the edge of the beautiful Cotswolds in Wotton-under-Edge, Gloucestershire.

Dancers, Salvador, Brazil. Peter Adams, UK

Monks on rickshaw, Inle, Burma. Peter Adams, UK

Worshippers at a mosque, Mumbai, India. Peter Adams, UK

Fisherman in his boat, Inle Lake, Burma. Peter Adams, UK

Fisherman cycling along the beach, Zanzibar, Tanzania. Peter Adams, UK

YOUNG TRAVEL PHOTOGRAPHER OF THE YEAR 2003

Chris Charnock's images of Venice and the Venetian islands were one of the first entries received in 2003 and are of a remarkably high standard. His shot of Florian's café (overleaf) is outstanding and would grace the pages of any book. At just 15 years old he is demonstrating great potential and the talent to merit the award of Young Travel Photographer of the Year.

Sponsors of this prize:

Light & Land   Fujifilm   Adobe   Lowepro

YOUNG TRAVEL PHOTOGRAPHER OF THE YEAR 2003

Chris Charnock UK
Winner

Chris Charnock, from Wigan, England, was 14 years old when he took his winning images, but has been a keen photographer since the age of 10. The son of professional photographers, he has already won an impressive batch of regional photographic club awards, but the title of Young Travel Photographer of the Year is his greatest success to date.

Chris hones his skills taking photographs of local football club Wigan Athletic in action, and is a regular photographic contributor to the sports pages of his local newspapers, the Wigan Observer, Wigan Reporter and Evening Post, where he hopes to work as a photojournalist in the future.

He took his winning images of Venice and Burano on a borrowed Fujifilm S2 Pro, ironically, the same model he went on to win as part of his Young Travel Photographer of the Year prize.

Florian Café, Venice, Italy. Chris Charnock, UK

Map reader, Venice, Italy. Chris Charnock, UK

Fishing nets in Burano, Venice, Italy. Chris Charnock, UK

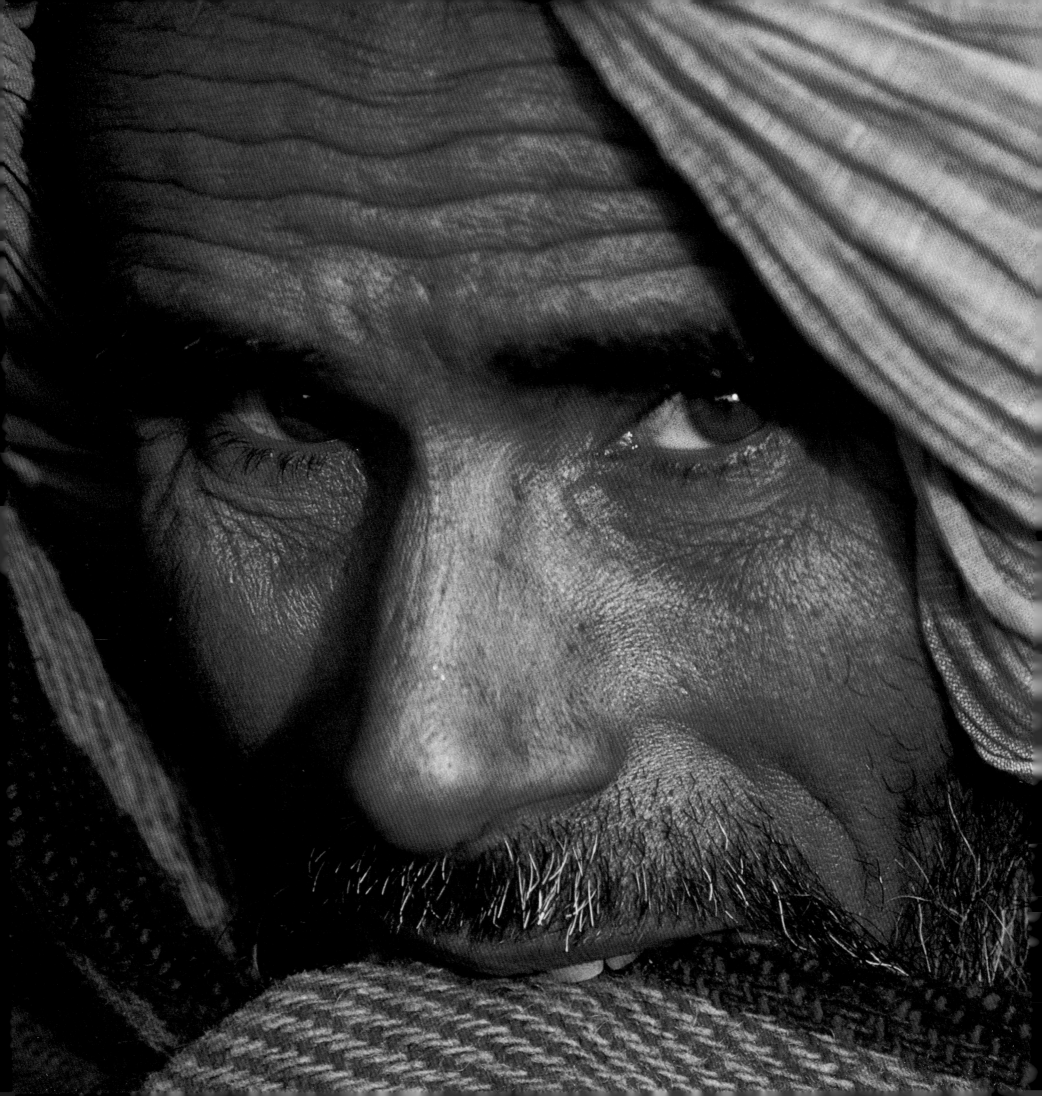

PEOPLE AND PLACES
PORTFOLIO 2003

Kurt Stier's winning images of Iran took on added poignancy with the devastating earthquake which hit the country one month after this award. The ancient city of Bam was virtually destroyed and tens of thousands of people lost their lives. Moments like these blur the lines between photographic genre, throwing travel and documentary photography together.

Sponsors of this prize:

Journey Latin America   Resolutions   Adobe   Lowepro

Red Burqa, Bandar Abbas, Iran. Kurt Stier, France

PEOPLE AND PLACES

Kurt Stier France
Winner

American-born, French-based Kurt Stier became interested in photography at a very early age, turning to photography when his childish attempts at painting and drawing became too frustrating and disappointing.

He has always drawn inspiration from a wide variety of sources – music, literature, and the arts. If he were to choose one photographer who inspired him directly, it would be Irving Penn, for whom he worked in the early '70s.

Kurt has been a professional photographer since leaving Penn Studio. He worked for some years in New York City doing fashion and still life, took a two-year hiatus in Vermont as a carpenter, then returned to photography and opened a studio in Boston, Massachusetts. Over the years in Boston, he worked in advertising, editorial, and corporate annual reports.

He now lives in France with his wife, the Iranian sculptor, Hourieh.

Kurt submitted the People and Places winning images of Iran because they are non-political and reflect a timeless quality of life in that ancient land.

Teahouse woman, Bam, Iran. This lady subsequently died in the terrible earthquake that devastated Bam in December 2003. Kurt Stier, France

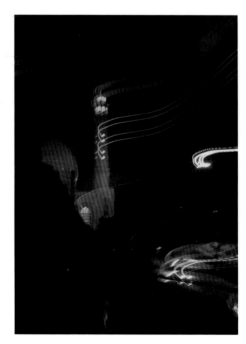

Minnaret, Qom, Iran. Kurt Stier, France

PEOPLE AND PLACES

Karoki Lewis UK
Runner Up

The images in Karoki Lewis' portfolio contrast dramatically in style with the category winner and the judges found it hard to decide between the two. Most striking of these images are the haunting and captivating portrait of a pilgrim (page 94) and this unusual image of the Taj Mahal. The latter is particularly impressive because this great monument has been photographed millions of times before. Karoki has found a different perspective, avoiding cliché with a stunningly beautiful image which captures the romance of the Taj Mahal yet contrasts this with the mundane demands of daily life.

Dhobis washing clothes in River Jamuna, Taj Mahal, Agra, India. Karoki Lewis, UK

Converted rice barge houseboat, Alleppey, Kerala, India. Karoki Lewis, UK

Tomb of Sufi saint, Salim Chishti, Fatehpur Sikri, India. Karoki Lewis, UK

Paradise Island, Malaysia. Pang Piow Kan, Malaysia

PEOPLE AND PLACES

Pang Piow Kan Malaysia
Highly Commended

These vibrant images of life in the stilt villages of the Malaysian islands are beautifully composed and uplifting. Clever use of angles adds to the dynamism of the images and draws you into them. You feel as if you are there too.

Paradise Island, Malaysia. Pang Piow Kan, Malaysia

Hampton Court Flower Show, London, England. Keith Bernstein, South Africa

PEOPLE AND PLACES

Keith Bernstein South Africa
Commended

Wow, what wonderful observation! Keith Bernstein's images just make you smile. This is very clever photography, precisely executed.

Scotland supporters at FIFA World Cup, Paris, France. Keith Bernstein, South Africa

SPIRIT OF ADVENTURE PORTFOLIO 2003

Adventure takes many forms. For some it is tackling the extremes of adversity, but for others it may be a relatively mundane task that challenges abilities. For category winner, Martin Hartley, adventure comes in the extreme form. His images capture the harshness of the Arctic environment and the challenges that it presents.

Sponsors of this prize:
Discover the World   Epson   Adobe   Lowepro

Pannirtung Fjord, Baffin Island. Martin Hartley, UK

SPIRIT OF ADVENTURE

Martin Hartley UK
Winner

Martin Hartley spent the end of 2003 in Antarctica, photographing British explorer Pen Hadow. At the start of 2003 Martin was working at the opposite end of the globe, photographing Hadow at the end of his record-breaking solo trek to the North Pole. Martin's pictures of the triumphant explorer were beamed around the world, and appeared in hundreds of national newspapers spread over dozens of countries.

Extraordinary journeys to the ends of the Earth were the last things on Martin's mind when he took his first photographic job, working for the UK Atomic Energy Authority, after completing his studies at the Bournemouth & Poole College of Art and Design. It was only a few years later, whilst working as a special effects photographer, that Martin entered a competition that was to change his life. His entry, delivered minutes before the deadline, led to an interview with a well-known British mountaineer, John Barry. Six months later, Martin found himself heading to Everest as an expedition photographer. He's never looked back.

On the rare occasions that Martin returns to his London home, he is quickly snapped up by clients who appreciate the extra dimension that he brings to corporate, advertising, editorial and studio photography.

Two adventurers in the back of a Komtik, King William Island. Martin Hartley, UK

Girl at local festival, Gjoa Haven, King William Island. Martin Hartley, UK

Expedition retracing the steps of Victorian explorer Sir John Franklin, King William Island. Martin Hartley, UK

Finchampstead, Berkshire, England. Martin Breschinski, UK

Piccadilly, London, England. Martin Breschinski, UK

Westminster Bridge, London, England. Martin Breschinski, UK

SPIRIT OF ADVENTURE

Martin Breschinski UK
Runner Up

What a wonderfully creative idea! Martin Breschinski used a self-made harness to strap his camera to his chest and a cable release in one hand to take these dramatic images. Although this is a very simple idea it's technically difficult to achieve. Martin should be applauded for thinking laterally in his interpretation of the spirit of adventure. The result is a portfolio of images that make you feel that you are personally involved in your own adventure. Feel the speed.

Somewhere between Canterbury and Rochester, Kent, England. Martin Breschinski, UK

SPIRIT OF ADVENTURE

Martin Hartley UK
Highly Commended

Timeless and exuberant are just two of the words that come to mind. Martin's Highly Commended and winning portfolios demonstrated two very different approaches to the theme. Would you ever tire of looking at images like these?

Skidoo sled, Swedish Lapland. Philip Lee Harvey, UK

SPIRIT OF ADVENTURE

Philip Lee Harvey UK
Commended

How cold did the photographer get taking these images? Philip Lee Harvey's portfolio is a beautifully composed documentary of daily life in one of the planet's more extreme environments.

Skier, Swedish Lapland. Philip Lee Harvey, UK

Morning market, Hoi An, Vietnam. Michael Matlach, USA

COLOUR AND PASSION PORTFOLIO 2003

Two words that encapsulate travel; colour and passion. Michael Matlach has used these to great effect in his winning portfolio. In soft light the subtle colours and movement give a real feel for the atmosphere of the early morning market, beautifully catching the dynamism of the scene.

Sponsors of this prize:

Guerba G.A.P Adventures Fujifilm Adobe Lowepro

Morning market, Hoi An, Vietnam. Michael Matlach, USA

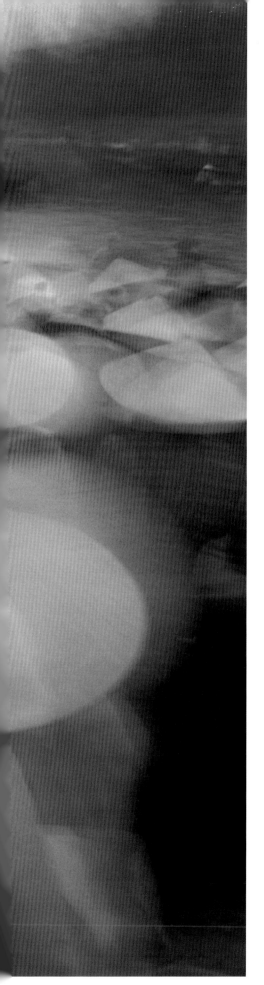

Morning market, Hoi An, Vietnam. Michael Matlach, USA

Morning market, Hoi An, Vietnam. Michael Matlach, USA

COLOUR AND PASSION

Michael Matlach USA
Winner

American Mike Matlach was always fascinated with images of far away places as shown in magazines such as National Geographic and Geographical. He initially expressed his love of adventure and the outdoors by becoming a fully certified ski instructor in the Rocky Mountains of Colorado. In his mid-twenties he obtained a degree in photography from Colorado Mountain College and pursued his goal of seeing the world through the camera lens. Early in his career he served as a technical assistant on assignment in South America for National Geographic, in Egypt for Life Magazine and in the Continental United States for Time Magazine.

Throughout his career, he has had a wide range of experience which includes architectural and sports photography, but he has found his true passion in photographing the people and cultures of the world.

Mike has developed and led tours to some of his favourite destinations such as Vietnam, Cambodia and India. His Colour and Passion winning images were taken in Hoi An, Vietnam, during the days preceding his wedding. He was married in a traditional Buddhist ceremony.

Chariot of the Gods, Penang, Malaysia. Sam Lim Kien Hock, Malaysia

COLOUR AND PASSION

Sam Lim Kien Hock Malaysia
Runner Up

Fabulous use of colour in both his crowd scenes and portraits captures a drama, excitement and joy of each moment in Sam Lim's images. The man on the mobile phone on the edge of the image above adds a fortuitous touch of humour and ironic comment on contemporary life.

Festival of Light, Penang, Malaysia. Sam Lim Kien Hock, Malaysia

Children under umbrella, Penang, Malaysia. Sam Lim Kien Hock, Malaysia

'We are the world', Penang, Malaysia. Sam Lim Kien Hock, Malaysia

Garlanded Naga Sadhu with axe during a Shahi Snaan, Maha Kumbh Mela, Allahabad, India. Karoki Lewis, UK

COLOUR AND PASSION

Karoki Lewis UK
Highly Commended

Karoki's entries, in this and other categories, have consistently demonstrated a high standard of photography. In this portfolio the different use of both static and dynamic elements of similar colour is particularly evocative and gives a real flavour of India.

Bhil tribal girl outside village dwelling, Jaisamund Lake, near Udaipur, Rajasthan, India. Karoki Lewis, UK

Indian shopkeeper, Port Blair, Andaman Islands. Martin Hartley, UK

Reading is a traditional part of Tibetan Buddhism – Incantations blend together to produce a hypnotic symphony, Zanskar, Northern India. Martin Hartley, UK

COLOUR AND PASSION

Martin Hartley UK
Commended

Although Martin won the Spirit of Adventure category with his portfolio of expedition photography, it is his low light portraiture which provides a particularly interesting and tranquil interpretation of the colour and passion of everyday life.

ESSENCE OF TRAVEL
SINGLE IMAGE 2003

What is the essence of travel? The sheer diversity of images shows a myriad of different interpretations that we have for this theme but Martin Brent's photograph must surely match an image that many envisage. However, far from cliché, it's beautifully executed and the panoramic format lends itself to the composition, or vice versa.

Sponsors of this prize:
Wacom   Adobe   Lowepro

ESSENCE OF TRAVEL

Martin Brent UK
Winner

Bromsgrove-based Martin Brent's images are well-known to the people of Birmingham, England, as one of the visual 'stars' of the re-branding of the city of Birmingham campaign. He has also completed a similar commission for the city of Hull.

Martin became interested in photography at the age of 10 and was an enthusiastic member of his school's photo club. On leaving school in 1984 he went on to study for an OND in photography. He became a freelance photographer's assistant and after a short time in a commercial studio assisted mainly on car advertising shoots until setting up on his own about nine years ago. He is a member of The Association of Photographers, London.

He discovered a love of travel photography after reaching a crossroads in his career and going travelling in the mid 1990s. He loves the opportunities it gives him to photograph local people and cultures, but remains conscious of the extremes of poverty he so often encounters. Consequently he makes a determined effort to do all he can to support the economies of the areas he visits. In 2004 he travelled to Australia to photograph the indigenous peoples of the Red Center for a new book.

Behind many great images lies a story and this is no exception. In the distance you can just make out a sand storm. Just after the image was taken, Martin was engulfed in the storm and his camera was ruined by the sand. Despite the sand getting into the back of the camera, the film was rescued and this was one of only six frames that survived.

Sahara Desert, Tunisia/Algeria border. The sandstorm that struck shortly after this picture was taken destroyed the camera used to take the shot. Martin Brent, UK

Fisherman, Zanzibar, Tanzania. Peter Adams, UK

ESSENCE OF TRAVEL

Peter Adams UK
Runner Up

Also part of Pete's winning Travel Photographer of the Year portfolios, this evocative image is timeless. Exposed to accentuate the light, pastel tones and capture just the right amount of movement; it's simply beautiful.

ESSENCE OF TRAVEL

Martin Hartley UK
Highly Commended

People featured highly in entrants' interpretation of the theme but this image stood out. There is something reminiscent of the Dutch master painters about it. Photography as art?

ESSENCE OF TRAVEL

David Hill UK
Commended

Childhood memories and the romance of steam echo a bygone age. Again there's a story behind Dave's commended image; having found the location earlier, but with no train due for a long time, Dave had travelled further along the coast. On hearing the train in the distance he doubled back and waited but the scene was engulfed by smoke from a bush fire. Frustration ensued as the train neared the bridge but at the very last second the wind changed and the train appeared through the smoke and haze. Right place, right time, some deserved luck and a great shot.

Stanzin and her mother, Padham, Zanskar Valley, India. Martin Hartley, UK

Steam, Kynsna, South Africa. David Hill, UK

Soldiers, Athens, Greece. Chris Parker, UK

Hiker on the dunes, Namibia. Alexandra Murphy, UK

Shadow in Djemmaa el Fna, Marrakech, Morocco. Juan Kratzmaier, Spain

2003 STUDENT AWARDS

A portrait, a landscape and a place provide three different styles from three different students. Brian Lockyer's portrait captures the joy of being young, while Sophie Tøndering's bicycle shot has an appealing, graphic, still life quality to it. The third winner, Krystyna Szulecka, captured an unusual and beautiful winter landscape from her native Poland.

Sponsors of this prize:
Plastic Sandwich

Christmas Eve, Czorsztyn, Poland. Krystyna Szulecka, UK

Bicycle in courtyard, Copenhagen, Denmark. Sophie Tøndering, Denmark

...And On

Yesterday morning we had a condor hovering over us as we waited for the dawn light, obviously tempted by the prospect of well-marinated meat. It looked bemused by our antics; we'd been doing the old YMCA bit to keep warm. Ever seen a bemused condor? They're like vultures on the ground, but majestic in flight and have been a constant theme to our Patagonian wandering.

We're camped by the lakeshore with the most dramatic view imaginable. There are numerous options for photographs at both dawn and dusk from within metres of our tent, it's a fantastic location. I love it when I can just stumble out of the tent at 5am and shoot locally.

Working here in Patagonia is quite a challenge though. The actual camera bit seems easy; the logistics of a trip like this are the hard part. The time spent by the tripod is a tiny part of the whole, being in the right place at the right time is the key. Food, water, fuel and shelter are luxuries easily taken for granted.

There is far, far more to this job than cameras and lenses.

David Noton — another day, another location

Cathedral reflection in pond. Gary Wornell, Finland

Churchgate Station, Bombay. Pete Pattisson, UK

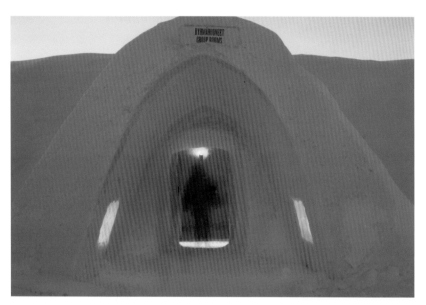

Snow Castle, Kemi, Finland. Tim Bird, Finland

Turkish girl, Ankara, Turkey. Robin Laurance, UK

Sufis spin in a dance that lasts for hours, Aleppo, Syria. Nicolas Randall, Spain

Iceberg in Jokulsarlon Glacial Lagoon, Skaftafell National Park, Iceland. Stephen Dean, UK

Rainbow over Rock of Cashel, Tipperary, Ireland. David Lyons, UK

Golden Gate Bridge, San Francisco, USA. Conor Caffrey, Ireland

Warriors, Masai Mara. Paul Goldstein, UK

Camels on dunes, Jaisalmer, India. H Satish, India

Volcano Lincancabur, Attacama Desert, Chile. Mark Chivers, UK

Song of Spring, Ansar, Sanpei, China. Pang Piow Kan, Malaysia

'Bedouin Aqua Girl', Nuwaibai, The Red Sea, Egypt. Chris Christoforou, UK

Two scooters, Colonia del Sacramento, Uruguay. Peter Netley, UK

Blue boy, Orissa, India. Kieron Nelson, Canada

Indian tourists on the beach, Andaman & Nicobar Islands. Lawrence Worcester, UK

Drying chilli peppers, Argentina. Michael Henchion, Ireland

Temple guardian, Bali. Tony Martorano, Australia

Huli men, Papua New Guinea. Derek Charlwood, UK

Tea, Morocco. Nina Assam, UK

Maasai playing cards, Ngorongoro Crater, Tanzania. Nicola Dove, UK

Gloria Velasquez, Nebaj, Guatemala. Jamie Marshall, UK

Salar de Uyuni, Bolivia. Jonathan Clay, UK

Lencois National Park, Brazil. Nigel Hillier, UK

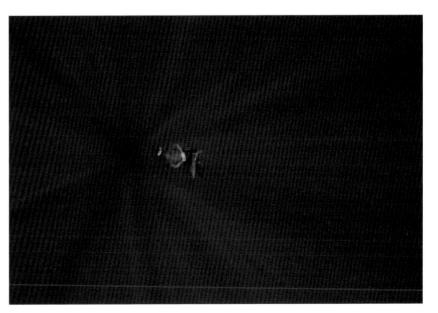

Free diver, Papua New Guinea. Shaun Tierney, UK

Abdul, Moheli, Comores. Daniel Clements, UK

Brazilian girls, Olinda, Brazil. Guy Moberly, Spain

Ama, Ghana. Marj Clayton, UK

Orthodox Jewish boys, Mea Shearim, Jerusalem, Israel. Nathan Briner, UK

Man on a bus, Delhi, India. Phil Dolby, UK

Red parasol from Padrao dos Descobrimento, Lisbon, Portugal. Martin Phillips, UK

Sunflower droplets, Pennsylvania, USA. Anupam Pal, USA

Venice Carnival, Venice, Italy. Marcus McAdam, UK

Gecko on a leaf, Thailand. John Aparicio, UK

Dyed chicks, New Year's Day festival, Madurai, India. Francine Lawrence, UK

Beach huts, Muizenberg, South Africa.
Martin Chamberlain, UK

Deer in Richmond Park, Surrey, England.
Jim White, UK

Camel's nose, Jaisalmer, Rajasthan, India. Kenton Mee, UK

Morning exercise, Hong Kong. Philip Lee Harvey, UK

Yoga, Englishman's Bay, Tobago. Richard Waite, UK

Pilgrim with holy water from the Sangon, Allahabad, India. Karoki Lewis, UK

Hat maker, Ecuador. Niall Riddell, UK

Postcards in Athens, Greece. Chris Parker, UK

Lovers, Via Condotti, Rome, Italy. Chris Etchells, UK

Old woman and chicken crossing the road, Highlands, Philippines. Jon Bower, UK

Fiat and Duomo, Florence, Italy. Martin Child, UK

Flamenco dancer, Santa Barbara's 'Old Spanish Days' celebration, California, USA. Lalove Benedict, USA

Music on the move, Trinidad, Cuba. Philip Lawson, UK

Food stall, Mataral, Bolivia. Krystyna Szulecka, UK

Dandelion, Ohio, USA. Virginia Gielow, USA

Weymouth beachfront, England. Simon Crofts, UK

Billboard, Calcutta, India. Lawrence Worcester, UK

Festive face, Grahamstown Festival, South Africa. Avi Hirschfield, Israel

The temple guardian, Penang, Malaysia. Sam Lim Kien Hock, Malaysia

Rastafarian, Jamaica. Matthew Wellings, UK

Dolphins, the shark-callers of Kontu, Papua New Guinea. George Blonsky, UK

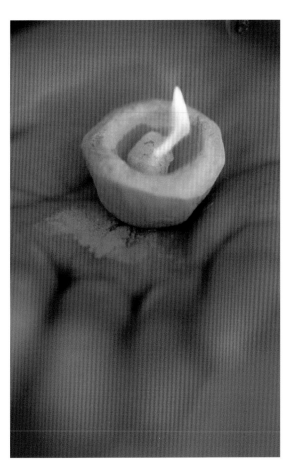

Worshipper holding offering, Prayag, Allahabad, India. Ras Powell Evans, UK

Restaurant, Manali to Leh Highway, Himachal Pradesh, India. Mike Hayes, UK

Maasai, Tanzania. Derek Charlwood, UK

Barn in USA. Terry McCreesh, Northern Ireland

Jaguar, Panatal, Brazil. Staffan Widstrand, Sweden

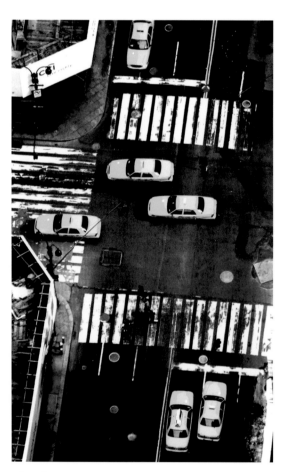

Yellow cabs, New York, USA. Chris Etchells, UK

Monk visiting The Bayon, Angkor, Cambodia. Jean-Christophe Godet, UK

Busy street scene, Thailand. Phil Cawley, UK

Rush hour, Grand Central Station, New York, USA. Ron Tear, UK

Early morning in Amfi, South India. Erez Biton, Israel

Brown bear, Alaska. Kennan Ward, USA

Sally Light Foot Crab, Galapagos Islands. Marco Pozzi, UK

Cricket at Shrewsbury School, England. Danny Beath, UK

Skateboarder, Waterloo Bridge, London, England. George Blonsky, UK

Seaweed, Stewart Island, New Zealand. David Hill, UK

The Huanghua Section of the Great Wall of China. Mike Stone, Australia

Retreat Room, Nangchen, Qinghai, China. Simon Lofting, UK

Rowing at Lake Velence, Hungary Wilmar Dik, Netherlands

Cuban diver feeding Bull Shark. Gavin Parsons, UK

Boogie boarders, Maui, Hawaii, USA. Michael Surowiak, UK

Sandy Lane, Barbados. Bob Thomas, UK

Climbers on Mont Blanc, French Alps. Martin Child, UK

Monk waiting for alms, Pattaya, Thailand. Henrietta Van den Bergh, UK

Olkhon Island, Lake Baikal, Siberia. Philip Lee Harvey, UK

Taj Mahal at dawn, India. Karoki Lewis, UK

Skiers, French Alps. Ron Tear, UK

JUDGES' FAVOURITES 2003

Travel Photographer of the Year is about great photography, and within many of the portfolios there were stunning individual images. The photographs on these pages are the judges' favourites from the 2003 entry.

Boy in trainers, Mali. Matjaz Krivic, Slovenia

Siberian dawn, Khatanga, Arctic Siberia. Martin Hartley, UK

This picture is wonderfully atmospheric and immediately takes me into another world. Wondering what it would be like to live in a place like this in a Siberian winter. I like the effort too, I'm sure the photographer stood around a while dreaming of tropical beaches to capture this. The small figure in the foreground gives the picture scale, human interest and adds some narrative. I almost feel as if I need to put on thermals just to look at this photograph.

Pete Adams, photographer and Travel Photographer of the Year 2003

Preparing the tea for the monks after meditation, Amdo, Eastern Tibet.
Alessandra Meniconzi, Switzerland

This image has a wonderful feel of a film still, all immaculately lit with crucial highlights spread throughout. There is the vaguest smile upon his face which betrays the "request" relationship of photographer to subject but no matter, the lighting and exposure are just so good.

Charlie Waite, landscape photographer, author and lecturer

Children playing on the road between Muang Phu Khun & Xiang Ngeun, Laos.
Felix Hug, Australia

I love this picture because of the happiness in the boy's face and the vitality of the image. This is a great portrait as well as an engaging travel photograph. It says something about the joy of childhood the world over and throughout the ages.

Debbie Ireland, Head of AA World Picture Library

JUDGES' FAVOURITES 2004

In 2004 each judge individually chose their own favourite image from the many thousands entered. Overleaf you'll find these images and the comments of the judge who selected them.

Images like this show the boundless ability of photography to capture every aspect of our world, celebrating both the vision and creativity of the photographers who took them.

Micoo girls, Guizhan, China. Jimmy Lam, USA

I find the mix of colour and movement very arresting. This is a wonderfully vibrant image that captures the essence of travel as if in a passing glimpse. It is the sort of picture I would be pleased to claim as my own!

Keith Wilson, editor – Outdoor Photography

Children march to school on opening day in Sapa, Vietnam. Mark Edward Harris, USA

The composition is superb, definitely a touch of Cartier-Bresson's decisive moment here. It's one of those pictures that make you want to go there. It's interesting how in this world of colour good black and white images stand out. This is the kind of image I look at and think 'I wish I'd shot that'.

David Noton, award winning travel and stock photographer

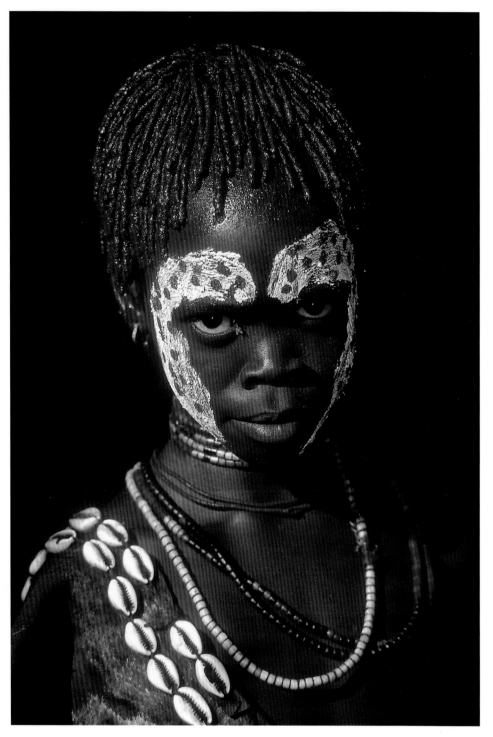

Baloo, Hamar Tribe, Ethiopia. Kieron Nelson, Canada

You feel the power of Africa through the eyes of this young boy's brilliantly framed portrait. The picture has a feel of one of the great master painters and yet brings a new way of looking at tribal imagery. The gaze is owned by the African warrior and we as the viewer are forced into a position of respect and awe of a world that is vanishing from our daily lives. The photographer has a clear understanding of story telling, incredible technical skill and an eye for the perfect moment.

Juliet Coombe, photojournalist, broadcaster and editor – Get Lost

Salar de Uyuni, Bolivia. Will Rolls, UK

I loved the sheer scale of this image: at first a fairly ordinary vast landscape, distant familiar horizon, and then these tiny figures draw you dramatically into the picture with their delicate placing in the composition. Questions turn this simple image into something special, as not only does the story behind the figures intrigue, but also the position of the photographer in order to gain such a great viewpoint. The simplicity of the colours in this image have been used to great effect to create enormous scale and distance, and of course it contains the finest essence of travel.

Nick Meers, photographer, author and lecturer

A boy plays near the entrance to the Rector's Palace, Dubrovnik, Croatia. Charles Round-Turner, UK

Great buildings witness many facets of human life yet seem to stand weathered but impervious to all that passes through them. In this image the stolid splendour of a beautiful building is brought together with the sheer exuberant vitality of a young boy and, for just one defining moment, static and dynamic are locked together. In capturing that moment the building comes alive and I find myself wishing that I was both that child and that photographer.

Chris Coe, photographer, author and lecturer

Hindu priest celebrating dawn at Chennai Beach, Tamil Nadu, India. Tony Martorano, Australia

Executives from Samsung take a break at Carribean Bay waterpark south of Seoul, Korea. Richard Sobol, USA

When I first saw this photograph on the judging table for the single image Celebration category, I immediately felt an over-whelming sense of calm, being engaged and seduced by the ceremonial painting of the face and beaded necklaces adorning the Hindu priest during prayer. Its simplicity transported me to another place.

A fabulous moment that I was able to appreciate and share with the photographer, Tony Martorano.

Terry Steeley, designer, digital imaging expert and lecturer

I think that this photo works on many different levels. Firstly, its unique cropping and composition are very effective – I really feel a part of the scene. I can imagine the heat of the hot sun and the cool water around their dangling fingers and toes. Secondly, the colour and light are wonderful. And thirdly, the contrast of opposing textures, the rippling water and the smooth floating rubber rings, really attract my attention. But I think I am most drawn to the photo for its sense of humour, irony, and play. It is a very contemporary perspective on culture, which I love.

Melissa De Witt, editor – Hotshoe

Tent on the slopes of Mount Kilimanjaro at dusk with the lights of Arusha visible below the clouds, Tanzania. Karoki Lewis, UK

Verreaux Sifaka, Berenty Reserve, Madagascar. Brian Matthews, UK

What makes the perfect travel photograph? For me, this outstanding image has it all – it captures a sense of freedom, discovery and natural wonder. A perfect moment frozen in time. It intrigues and delights the eye. The 'illuminated tent' in the foreground provides a warm human element in an expansive sky where night gives way to day and the mountain vista seems to stretch to eternity. Beautifully shot and sensitively composed; this image is both thought-provoking and visually stunning!

Mark Banister, digital and film retoucher

Talented photographers manage to capture great moments while maintaining all of the technical aspects of colour, lighting, focus and composition within the image. This image captures the joy of nature and relates an intimate view of movement that seems quite human. The balance of dark and light colours linked with the depth of field that pushes the background into a soft muted backdrop is as much an art form as it is a pleasure. When you see a primate what words come to mind? Swinging, jumping, climbing, leaning, crazy maybe even clowning. In this case a picture is worth a thousand words.

Michael O'Neill, digital imaging expert

PHOTOGRAPHIC SPONSORS

ADOBE

Adobe helps people and businesses communicate better through its world-leading digital imaging, design and document technology platforms for consumers, creative professionals and enterprises. Adobe's revenue in its last fiscal year exceeded $1.2 billion.

www.adobe.co.uk

CALUMET

Calumet is the leading 'three-tailer' (retail, mail order and e-commerce) for photography, digital imaging, studio equipment, and professional audio/visual products. Its unrivalled level of experience and knowledge of the marketplace make it one of the most respected global suppliers.

www.calumetphoto.com

FUJIFILM

If you take a look at the best travel photography, the chances are, most of it will be on Fujifilm. Wherever travel photography happens, Fujifilm is never far off. Whether you choose from award-winning slide films or portable, creative digital cameras, there will always be an element of 'green' to travel photography. Fujifilm is committed to developing the very best photographic products, both conventional and digital. Fuji Photo Film (UK) Ltd has been supplying the imaging, printing and graphics industries, as well as professional and enthusiast photographers, with high quality, innovative products and services for more than 25 years.

www.fujifilm.co.uk

HASSELBLAD (UK) Limited

For over fifty years Hasselblad has been committed to providing exciting cameras of outstanding quality and reliability to discerning photographers. Each and every Hasselblad product reflects core values of superior image quality, reliability and pleasure of handling. The Hasselblad range now includes the world's first integrated digital medium format camera: the Hasselblad H1D! High-End digital capture backs and a wide range of scanners round off a unique programme of products, designed for the most demanding image makers. Whether it's film or digital, Hasselblad products help you achieve your true potential!

www.hasselblad.co.uk

HEWLETT PACKARD

HP is the digital photography expert, with everything a hobbyist or professional could want or need. With everything from the Photosmart range of desktops and notebooks to scanners and printers, and of course the cameras themselves, HP has a range for everyone. HP has channelled its extensive experience in imaging and printing into the development of these award-winning and market-leading products, so photographers know they're getting the best results, whether shooting, sharing or editing.

www.hp.com/uk

Kids, South Africa. Hannah Timm, UK.

PLASTIC SANDWICH

Plastic Sandwich has been putting together portfolios for photographers and art directors since the early 1970s. Plastic Sandwich has clients all over the world, in fact wherever there is a photographic industry. Amongst its clients are the household names and stars of the industry, plus their assistants and students, who find the advice the company can offer of great help. Plastic Sandwich's services are also utilised by companies such as event organisers, PR organisations and anyone whose activities or craft are best shown through the presentation of images. Joyce and Rob are available to discuss any presentation ideas or problems.

www.plasticsandwich.co.uk

RESOLUTIONS

Delivery of key messages in an entertaining and stimulating way is paramount in this overcrowded information age. Resolutions' solutions are designed to deliver effective presentations, video and interactive training programmes across a range of media such as video, CD-ROM, DVD and the web. No matter what the medium, Resolutions can deliver the key message in an interactive and engaging way.

www.resolutionsuk.com

WACOM

Founded in 1983, Wacom has established itself as the market leader in pen based digital imaging and is a pioneer in the development of the pen as an input device for computers. The company's products are based on its patented 'Penabled technology', meaning that all its input devices are cordless, battery-less and pressure sensitive. Wacom's current range of pen tablets is ideal for professional and amateur users alike. For digital imaging and photography, it provides advanced functionality for improved workflow and productivity. The pen offers unparalleled levels of control and precision, which is particularly effective for instance, when retouching photographs or masking.

www.wacom-europe.com

Horseman of the highlands, Litang, Tibetan Plateau. Will Salter, Australia

TRAVEL SPONSORS

ISLANDS OF THE BAHAMAS

From centuries-old mansions and deserted, bright white sand beaches of Long Island, and the mythical charm and tranquil beauty of Andros, to cosmopolitan Nassau with its duty-free shops, golf, museums and restaurants, each of the 700 islands of The Bahamas has its own distinct personality. But all offer spectacular scenery, a glorious climate, vivid blue warm tropical waters, an abundance of fascinating wildlife and beautiful flora and friendly, welcoming people. It's easy to understand why generations of photographers, wildlife enthusiasts, golfers, big game fishermen and holidaymakers have found that the hardest part is deciding which Islands to visit!

www.bahamas.co.uk

DISCOVER THE WORLD

Discover the World, one of the UK's leading specialist tour operators, offers a range of unique specialist holidays through six different worldwide travel programmes. From tailor-made independent holidays to escorted tours, wildlife experiences to adventurous expeditions and leisurely fly-drive touring, there is something to suit every budget and taste. Their imaginative itineraries ensure travellers get the most out of each destination and their in-depth specialist knowledge of all the countries to which they operate, means the diverse selection of holidays never fails to impress. Destinations include Iceland, Greenland, Sweden, Lapland, New Zealand, the Arctic, Antarctica, the Bahamas and many more.

www.discover-the-world.co.uk

G.A.P ADVENTURES

G.A.P Adventures has 14 years of expertise travelling all over Latin America (where we have more departures than any other adventure operator) and around the world. When we say small groups we mean it; most tours have a maximum size of 12 travellers and are suited for people with a lust for life and a curiosity for culture, wildlife and nature. In 2004 G.A.P purchased the legendary ship 'The Explorer' and is now able to venture further off the beaten track, from Antarctica to the Arctic and up the mighty Amazon!

www.gapadventures.com

GUERBA

For 25 years Guerba has been at the forefront of adventure travel, offering exciting adventure and discovery holidays to Asia, Africa, South America, Europe and the Antarctic. Guerba works with local operators with established ecotourism standards. Fundraising efforts to build a school and now an orphanage near Kilimanjaro in Africa have led to the 2004 best mountain operator award for responsible tourism. The company has a singles policy to avoid compulsory single supplements on most adventures, and the experienced tour leaders bring out the best in small group adventures. Guerba shows you the world 'in close-up'.

www.guerba.com

LAND ROVER

Off-road, on-road and on-film Land Rover continues to create legendary vehicles that deliver excitement to generations of adventurers. As the UK's leading 4x4 manufacturer, Land Rover's story is marked by innovation and off-road design excellence, from the original Land Rover launched in 1948 to the latest award-winning Range Rover. Land Rovers are a must for intrepid photographers with a pioneering spirit who need to reach remote landscapes, cross rugged ravines or climb muddy inclines to capture those award-winning shots. Land Rover works with global conservation partner Biosphere Expeditions to participate in ecological preservation projects.

www.landrover.com   www.biosphere-expeditions.org

LIGHT AND LAND

Light & Land is Britain's premier provider of photographic tours and workshops. They have the widest choice of destinations and themes; they run over 60 photographic courses a year to destinations in the UK, Europe, America and as far afield as Antarctica and Mongolia; the themes covered range from architecture to landscape, from large format to the digital darkroom and from portraiture to wildlife. Light & Land's team of tutors includes many of Britain's top professional landscape and wildlife photographers, with famous names such as Joe Cornish, Heather Angel, David Ward and Charlie Waite.

www.lightandland.co.uk

STAR ALLIANCE

By bringing together fifteen of the world's finest airlines we've created a unique and easier travelling experience. It offers all the flexibility you need and reduces hassle. We've even harmonised timetables to make your connections smoother. Whichever Star Alliance member airline you fly with, we've made sure your journey is as rewarding as it is relaxing. And we encourage our airlines to preserve and promote their own unique traditions and cultures. We are Air Canada, Air New Zealand, ANA, Asiana Airlines, Austrian, bmi, LOT Polish Airlines, Lufthansa, SAS, Singapore Airlines, Spanair, Thai Airways International, United Airlines, US Airways and VARIG. Together, we give you what no one airline could.

www.staralliance.com

TRIBES TRAVEL

TRIBES, the Fair Trade Travel company, aims to offer holidays which are not only second to none in terms of quality and excitement, but which are also of benefit to the local people, environment and wildlife of the destination you choose to travel to. Tribes has put together a comprehensive and unique collection of trips in 14 countries, covering cultural holidays, wildlife journeys and safaris, trekking trips, special interest holidays, short breaks and some wonderful areas for pure relaxation. The holidays are mostly tailor-made specifically for clients, though there is also a selection of group trips on set dates.

www.tribes.co.uk

The "wave" at North Coyote Buttes, Arizona, USA. Daisy Gilardini, Switzerland

CREATIVE SPONSORS

AVERY DENNISON

Founded in 1935, Avery Dennison is the global leader in pressure-sensitive technology and innovative self-adhesive solutions for consumer products and label materials. Throughout the world Avery Dennison develops, manufactures and markets a wide range of products for consumer and industrial markets, including Avery-brand office products, Fasson-brand self-adhesive materials, peel-and-stick postage stamps, automated retail tag and speciality tapes and chemicals. In the UK, Avery Dennison Office Products is the world's leading manufacturer of self-adhesive labels for laser and inkjet printers, labelling software, filing, indexing, office accessories, cutters & quillotines and other office, home and school related supplies.

www.avery.co.uk

CONNEKT COLOUR

Connekt Colour, the print division of the Technik group, delivers brilliant print and faultless, calm untroubled service. Continual investment in technology and people allows Connekt to respond to the needs of its clients - whatever the message, however complex the job, however difficult or unusual the treatment, Connekt meets the challenge. Its high level of customer retention reflects Connekt's consistent delivery of quality and service; the Connekt team works alongside clients to understand their business, and offers honest opinions and straightforward advice, developing an excellent working partnership with no hidden surprises. This book – printed by Connekt Colour – is a testament to Connekt's very high production standards.

www.connektcolour.com

Exhibition • Brochure • Design • Print

EXPOSURE

Exposure designs and produces brochures, exhibitions and graphics, from photographing the product to the end result. In addition, our other services include digital printing, retouching and project management as well as a host of other related services. Exposure's enthusiasm is testament to the professional quality and determination of the team here. We offer overall commitment to customers by providing top quality products and top quality service. Listening to what our clients want and making sure they are completely satisfied is our only priority.

www.exposure.uk.net

Blacktip Reefshark, Kuramathi Island, Maldives. Felix Hug, Australia

Travel Photographer of the Year would like to thank all of our sponsors for their support, and acknowledge the invaluable role that they have played in the foundation and growth of the competition. Without them it would not have been possible to launch the competition or establish it as the premier showcase for travel photography.

We would also like to thank Epson, Journey Latin America and Lowepro for sponsoring Travel Photographer of the Year in its first year.

Chukchi Pjotr Peneteovi, Chukotka, Siberia. Staffan Widstrand, Sweden

Four wheel driving, Iceland. David Vintiner, UK

INDEX OF PHOTOGRAPHERS

Snowy square, Kiev, Ukraine. Iain Bain, UK

Camera from a piece of a Sagu tree, rain forest, Mentawai, Indonesia. Remi Benali, France